S0-APQ-114

ANMARIE BARRIE

For Mom:
Who Gave Everything
And Asked For Nothing.
                    A.B.

A Beginner's Guide to
Budgerigars

Written By
Anmarie Barrie

Contents

© 1986 by T.F.H. Publications, Inc. Distributed in the UNITED STATES by T.F.H. Publications, Inc., 211 West Sylvania Avenue, Neptune City, NJ 07753; in CANADA by H & L Pet Supplies Inc., 27 Kingston Crescent, Kitchener, Ontario N2B 2T6; Rolf C. Hagen Ltd., 3225 Sartelon Street, Montreal 382 Quebec; in ENGLAND by T.F.H. Publications Limited, 4 Kier Park, Ascot, Berkshire SL5 7DS; in AUSTRALIA AND THE SOUTH PACIFIC by T.F.H. (Australia) Pty. Ltd., Box 149, Brookvale 2100 N.S.W., Australia; in NEW ZEALAND by Ross Haines & Son, Ltd., 18 Monmouth Street, Grey Lynn, Auckland 2 New Zealand; in SINGAPORE AND MALAYSIA by MPH Distributors (S) Pte., Ltd., 601 Sims Drive, #03/07/21, Singapore 1438; in the PHILIPPINES by Bioi-Research, 5 Lippay Street, San Lorenzo Village, Makati Rizal; in SOUTH AFRICA by Multipet Pty. Ltd., 30 Turners Avenue, Durban 4001. Published by T.F.H. Publications, Inc. Manufactured in the United States of America by T.F.H. Publications, Inc.

1.
Introduction

Budgerigars are the best known species of parrot. Commonly referred to as a parakeet in the United States, this term is actually a misnomer, since there are other parakeets that are not Budgerigars.

Of the approximately 340 species of parrots, half are found in Australia and the Pacific islands, 140 in Central and South America and the Caribbean, and the remainder in Africa and southern Asia.

Parrots have hooked bills, a comparatively large skull, a thick tongue, special feathers called powder downs, and feet with two toes facing forward and two facing backward.

Native to Australia, Budgerigars are commonly found in large flocks throughout the interior grasslands. Their migration follows the availability of water, seeding grasses, and favorable weather. Eucalyptus groves are their favorite roosts, particularly trees with holes. From there they fly off to feed on seeds, sprouts, plant shoots, and flower parts.

Being very social, Budgerigars are colony breeders. Nesting sites will be only a few feet apart throughout a tree, even in the roots. Breeding is not seasonal, but dependent rather on a combination of age and good health. As long as food is available and the weather permits, Budgerigars will breed continually.

Wild birds are smaller and slimmer than captive-bred budgies. Domestic birds average 8-1/2 inches in length from tip of beak to tail. The natural coloring is a luminous green, with a yellow facial mask. Black and yellow markings form a wavy barring on the wings, nape of neck, and the back of the head. Tail feathers are edged in blue, and violet blue patches are apparent on the cheeks. A chain of six black spots decorates the throat.

Females are dominant in the species. They have a powerful bite from strong beak muscles that are used in preparing a nest. Neither parent, though, will easily abandon its brood.

The average life of a budgie is six to fifteen years.

2.
Budgies as pets

Budgies have a striking appearance. In addition, they are alert, intelligent, and inquisitive. Being social animals, they solicit attention and may come to enjoy being picked up and stroked. Their small size, cleanliness, and hardiness make them ideal pets.

Being extremely docile and long-lived, Budgies are well suited to life in captivity. They require minimum space and a simple diet. Their ease of care, willingness to breed, and low cost make them good pets for beginners learning the basics of birds.

Budgies are attractive and come in a variety of colors: they are competent imitators of the human voice and other sounds; they require little time for training and are easy to handle. They are clean and need little maintenance, are easily transported, and have great personalities. They are a long lasting source of entertainment, adapt readily to changes in environment, breed willingly, and pose no harm. They can be kept safely out of the way, have a low initial purchase cost, and subsequent expenses are minimal.

Disadvantages are important considerations when purchasing any pet. Budgerigars are susceptible to drafts and sensitive to changes in their diet. If you are planning an extended trip, a reliable friend needs to visit the bird every other day to replenish the food and water. The cage requires cleaning, and the bird should be allowed to fly for exercise.

There are no records of a Budgie being housebroken. Droppings may be found throughout the flying area. Since Budgies have strong instinct, furniture and other items may be gnawed as the bird explores.

Some Budgies are quite verbal. They may make noise at inopportune times. They may also repeat words or phrases that are quite unexpected.

Buying your bird

A variety of stores sell birds and pets. A pet shop or bird store with experienced, reliable employees should be selected when buying your bird. Choose a dealer with good inventory and clean, neat cages. Seek out employees who can offer sound advice.

A very beautiful colored Budgie. This color is called opal cobalt. Photo by Harry V. Lacey.

Now it is time to select a bird. Choose a Budgie with a sleek, well-groomed look. The plumage should be full and healthy. Avoid a bird with ruffled feathers or watery eyes and nostrils. The Budgie should be bright-eyed, alert and inquisitive. Stand back from the cage to avoid interfering with natural behavior, and observe the bird for a time. It should display an active interest in its food and

When you select your bird at the petshop, look for a Budgie that has a sleek, well-groomed look, with full, healthy plumage. Don't mistake colored blotches with disease. This is natural in some color varieties. Photo by Michael Gilroy.

socialize with its cage mates. The Budgie should be playful, not sitting alone. Note any prolonged periods of lethargy.

A puffed-up and tired look can mean the bird is sleepy, but it can also be a sign of illness. A healthy Budgie will sleep on one leg, an ill bird will remain on two.

Handle the bird in the store and thoroughly examine it. The breast should feel firm, plump, and full. There should be no bare spots on the body. The feathers should be clean, not soiled around the vent, an indication of diarrhea. The droppings must be firm, not loose and watery, and a mixture of black and white—not yellow, green, or brown. Do not accept a bird with sores or wounds.

12

The Budgie's mandibles should come together nicely and not be deformed.

Budgies come in a wide variety of color mutations: pied, lutino, lacewings, cinnamon, and others. If you cannot find a suitable bird, the right color combination can probably be ordered.

This is dangerous! The Budge could easily take a nasty bite from the dog's nose . . . or the dog could eat the bird. There are many cases where birds and dogs have become friends, but it is dangerous. Teach your child about this danger.

If you are planning to tame the bird, buy only one. Additional birds will be more interested in each other and therefore more difficult to tame. If you do not have the desire to tame, two can be purchased and they may still develop a friendship with people. Or, you may be lucky enough to find a shop that offers birds already hand-tamed.

If you do not intend to breed the birds and you buy two, be sure they are males. This will avoid the pair surprising you by breeding. Since females are dominant, they will be less compatible than males. The females may fight more seriously. With their stronger beaks, more damage can be inflicted.

Taming is more easily accomplished with young birds five to six weeks old. If you want the birds for immediate breeding, then around one year of age is desirable, even though the birds mature sexually earlier.

Budgies mature at around nine months. Immature birds are more dull than adults, their coloring is not as intense. The markings are incomplete, and they exhibit striping on the forehead. The eyes are totally dark.

With the first molt, the forehead bars fade. The iris turns lighter, usually yellow, and the pupil remains dark. The cere (the fleshy area above the beak) also changes color. Initially pink in males, the cere darkens to blue or purple. Females are bluish and turn tan, deepening to brown when breeding. The beak itself is blackish in the young, turning yellowish with maturity.

Cages

Budgies are used to wide-open spaces, so choose a cage with plenty of room. A cage that is too confining could also damage a bird's feathers and subsequently cause a decline in health. If for some reason a small cage is necessary, allow your pet daily flights for exercise. A good size is about two cubic feet.

Select a rectangular metal cage with horizontal wires about three-eighths to three-quarters of an inch apart. A favorite pastime of the Budgie is climbing up and down the sides of its cage. Having the wires close together prevents the bird from entrapping its head between them. And because Budgies are avid chewers, a wooden cage would soon need to be replaced.

One of the most difficult tasks in taming is moving the bird in and out of the cage. Therefore, the door should be large enough for you to remove the bird while it rests on your hand without having to touch any part of the cage. Some cages even have doors of various sizes. Others allow the top to be removed so the Budgie can exit and enter at will.

This grey-green combination Budgie is a very rare but beautiful color. Photo by Harry V. Lacey.

Decide where in the house the cage will be kept. Eye level is preferred because the bird will feel more secure. In the wild, danger (predatory birds) comes from above. If the cage is too high, the birds will be denied sufficient human contact. So, whether the cage will be hung or placed on a table or stand is an important consideration.

Cages usually come with seed and water containers, but plastic or ceramic dishes can be used as well. Place them on the floor of the cage away from any perches to prevent contamination from droppings. There are cages available that provides places for dishes to be hung from the side of the cage. This avoids tipping and lessens the chance of droppings ending up in them. It is likely that such a cage will also have individual doors for each dish to facilitate cleaning and refilling.

Budgies feed by cracking open seeds. The shed hulls are dropped back in the dish. These accumulate on top of the remaining seed and need to be removed daily. Some birds will not find the food underneath the hulls. Seed hoppers can be used instead of open dishes. Seed hoppers have drawers that catch the hulls and can be emptied. This means that the seed is partially covered. Be sure your bird is capable of finding the food when a hopper is used.

Do not crowd your Budgie with accessory items. If the cage does not come with a perch, select two or three in natural wood in varying sizes, to exercise the feet and legs. Toys, bells, and mirrors can be clipped in the cage for amusement. Do not use string or chain in which a Budgie can become entangled and injure itself. Table-tennis balls or a branch from a tree that can be chewed and splintered are great fun. Be creative and periodically change the toys.

Line the cage floor with paper. If there is a cage grate, sand or gravel paper can be used for extra absorbency. The grate prevents the Budgie from eating the soiled sand and becoming ill. It also keeps the bird from walking in its droppings. Replace the litter every two to three days or whenever the mess makes you uncomfortable. Some cages come with a sliding tray that facilitates cleaning. In others, the wire top may be detached from the bottom and can be placed on the floor or a mat.

Wash and dry the cage bottom weekly, and periodically wash the cage bars. Scrubbing with a stiff brush will loosen any dried debris.

A cage need not be filled with accessory items. Too much "junk" and the bird won't have any room (though they don't require much if they are allowed out of the cage). Make sure you include a Nylabird pacifier for the bird to chew on when it gets the urge to chew. Photo by Norma Veitch.

Clean the perches with a brush, fine sandpaper, or a perch scraper. Let them dry completely before placing them back in the cage. Wet perches can cause arthritis, rheumatism, and colds. The food and water dishes need to be washed daily with hot water and soap.

For the first few days, the cage should be in a quiet room, like a spare bedroom. This is only meant to be temporary, until the bird settles in. After a short time, move it permanently to a more active room. Avoid kitchens where drastic temperature changes are common. Average daytime temperatures should be between 65 and 80 degrees. Nighttime can be as low as the high 40s.

Place the cage in an area that is free of smoke and well ventilated, but away from drafty windows and doors. Captive birds have a thinner coat of down and so are more susceptible to chills. Avoid heaters and radiators that can be drying, thereby damaging the feathers.

Be sure the cage is protected from prolonged exposure to sunlight; an area of indirect natural light is best.

A Budgie is used to a twelve-hour day. At night, the room should be quiet and dark. If this is not possible, a drape or cloth placed over the cage will do as well. The Budgie needs its rest. This cloth can also serve to calm the bird should it become noisy or anxious. When it has quieted down, remove the drape. Do not keep it covered, for it may just have been trying to get your attention.

Budgies live in arid regions and are not used to bathing. They usually roll in the damp grass. Therefore, providing a bathing dish is not mandatory, but it can be tried. As an alternative, place some wet lettuce or grass on the cage floor.

If you would like to bring your caged Budgie outside, remember that the cage has highly reflective properties. Hang the cage from a tree out of direct sunlight and away from potential predators. It is safe to have the cage on the ground only if the area is free of danger and there is constant supervision. Your bird is a helpless victim. It cannot flee from any harm that may present itself.

This is a light grey opaline color. **Photo by Harry V. Lacey.**

19

Bringing your new pet home

The Budgie will probably be placed in a box so that you can bring it home. Have the cage prepared in advance so that the time your bird spends in the box will be lessened.

During transport, keep the bird warm. The journey will be shock enough, so try to avoid any additional trauma. Do not move the bird on a cold, windy, or damp day. This will decrease the chance of your bird becoming ill.

You may want to take the bird to a vet that same day. Arrange with the shopkeeper to exchange the bird if the vet says it is unfit. If possible, bring the bird home early in the day to allow it time to adjust before dark. This also gives you time to reexamine the bird at home after it has had some time to settle in and recuperate from the stress of transport. If it seems ill, do not hesitate to call the shopkeeper. The longer the delay, the less responsibility will be taken by him. Do not be alarmed, though, if your bird remains motionless for prolonged periods. It may eat very little the first few days. This is a normal reaction.

An untame bird may quiver when it is watched. Sometimes a sign of illness, for your new arrival it merely indicates an unfamiliarity with human contact.

You may be a little hesitant to handle the bird if you lack experience. Remember that the bird is more afraid of you. Use a firm but gentle touch to take the bird out of the box and place it in the cage. To protect you from a painful bite, wear a pair of thin cotton gloves, or wrap your fingertips with adhesive strip or tape. Gloves that are bulky may frighten the bird even more.

Never grip the bird by the throat; always support the full weight of its body. Grasping it by the tail feathers will leave you with a handful of feather but no bird! If the bird does fly free, simply capture it with a net or a light towel or cloth.

For the first week or two, do not attempt to handle the bird. Speak to the bird, but don't create a disturbance. Depending on the bird's disposition, it may sit quietly or restlessly twitch and move its tail. The bird was probably used to an abundance of social contact at the shop, and now it is all alone.

It is more difficult to train two Budgies than one. Two Budgies will play with each other rather than with you!

Use your own judgment to determine when the bird is ready for training. Each bird will respond at its own pace.

If a bird is housed alone for a long time, a couple of years, it may not accept a new bird. Keep this in mind if you plan to expand eventually. Single birds may also lose their natural interest in breeding.

Feeding

A balanced diet and plenty of exercise circumvents many diseases and breeding disorders. Diseases have a more deleterious effect on a poorly nourished body. Provide your Budgie with a variety of seeds, greens, and animal protein.

Commercial Budgie, or parakeet, food usually contains canary seed, oats, niger, hemp, poppy, sunflower, and millet. If you decide to mix your own, blend 30–40% canary seed, 40–50% millet, and 5% of niger, linseed, poppy, and lettuce seeds. Your bird's digestive system will extract almost every nutrient available in the seed.

Oats are fattening, so do not give them regularly to your bird. Bread is of little nutritional value and is also fattening. Too much will cause the Budgie to overeat in order to compensate for the lack of nutrients. It will appear bloated, but will actually be undernourished.

Local weeds and grasses (especially chickweed) not treated with insecticides are a good source of greens. Lettuce, spinach, dandelion leaves, watercress, celery, and peas are easily obtainable throughout the year. Fruits such as apples, oranges, and bananas can be cut up and pushed between the bars of the cage for your bird to eat. These are best provided in the morning, then removed before they sour.

In the late afternoon a Budgie is likely to fill up on solids for the night. It is a good idea not to leave fresh foods overnight because they may be spoiled by morning. Wilted, rotten foods are dangerous. A rule of thumb is to not feed your bird anything that is not as fresh as what you yourself would eat.

Fresh branches from trees and bushes (willow, poplar, and fruit trees) satisfies the Budgie's gnawing instinct while providing good nutrition. Be sure to wash all food before offering it to your pet.

It may take some time for your bird to accept a new food, but it should always be made available. Allow the bird to pick and choose according to its own individual tastes. You may find that it will be more receptive to lighter-colored foods.

Hard-boiled eggs, meat, fish, liver, soybeans, and cheese are all recommended sources of protein and fat. Introduce any new foods gradually, not too many at one time. A Budgie's system can be easily upset by changes.

A Budgie gets most of its water from the fresh, juicy greens, but drinking water should always be present. Your bird will drink it occasionally. Once or twice a week fortify the water with a liquid vitamin supplement. Choose one that contains the vitamin-B complex.

This is a very desirable color . . . the cobalt Budgerigar. The large dots on the throat are very rare and very desirable from a Bird Show point of view. Photo by Harry V. Lacey.

These birds are typical of very high quality show Budgies. They have large throat dots, full heads and the greens, blues and greys are uniform in color. Photo by Harry V. Lacey.

Your petshop will have a great variety of accessories which your Budgie might find entertaining. Budgies are natural climbers, so things which make it climb will be most appreciated.

During molting and while breeding, a few drops of cod liver oil or wheat germ oil added to some seed is advisable. Keep this seed in a separate dish from the regular seed. Too much is fattening.

Periodically, your bird may display courtship behavior. It will regurgitate as if feeding a mate. The bird is not ill, and this activity will soon stop.

You may wish to sprout your own grasses from seed. Simply wet the seed and place it on a damp paper towel. If it does not sprout, then it is not a good food dry either. The seed should taste sweet, not bitter. These are two tests to determine the nutritional value of the seed.

A properly cared for bird will be healthy. A poor diet may lead to illness. After your bird has calmed down and developed a routine, monitor its food intake over a week. Be aware of how much and what kinds of food it consumes. In the future, you will be able to note any changes that may indicate illness. Sometimes the bird may eat more, such as during molting or cold weather, in an effort to maintain its body temperature.

No more than a three to four week supply of seed should be kept on hand, in order to avoid spoilage. Seal it in moisture-proof containers in the refrigerator or some other cool, dry place. Moisture and humidity may foster molds, which will make the bird ill. Also, with time, the seed can dry out and lose its nutritional value.

If you follow this routine, there will be no need for special foods, tonics, or conditioners.

Grit and cuttlebone

Grit contains essential minerals and elements for your pet. It is stored in the gizzard as an aid in digestion, especially of seed. The grit, or bird sand, should include charcoal, and ideally some other organic material, such as oyster shells or barnacles. If it does not, these can be bought separately and added to the grit. Crushed eggshells are a good substitute. These organic compounds are especially important during breeding. Keep the grit mixture in a dish separate from the regular food, and replace it weekly.

Nylabird parrot pacifiers are a must for every parrot bird (yes, a Budgie is also a parrot). The nylon is filled with oystershell calcium which keeps the bird's beak in trim. It also satisfies the chewing need!

Budgies are very inquisitive birds. They chew on anything which shines. If you are lucky enough to have a diamond bracelet, make sure your pet Budgie doesn't loosen one of the stones!

Cuttlebone is the internal shell of the cuttlefish, a marine animal closely related to squid. It provides calcium for a firm beak, strong eggshells when breeding, and also prevents egg binding. During breeding, its consumption may be doubled. Gnawing on the cuttlebone, or a similar mineral block, helps to keep the beak from becoming overgrown.

Cuttlebone usually comes with a clip. If it has none, simply punch holes in it and attach it with wire to the side of the cage near a perch.

What a magnificent bird! This surely is a champion. It is called a banded pied cobalt Budgie. Photo by Harry V. Lacey.

30

3.

Taming

Clipping your new pet's wing feathers will make taming easier. Taming can still be done without clipping, but it will be considerably more tiring for you and the bird. Clipping the wing feathers means that the Budgie will have limited ability to fly. It will lose its balance and have to land after traveling only a few feet. When the bird is let out of the cage, there is no possibility of its escaping.

An almost perfect head on a show-quality
Budgie. Photo by Harry V. Lacey.

Done properly, wing clipping is quick, easy, and painless for your bird. It can be done by one person, but it is easier with two: one holds the bird while the other clips. It's best to watch someone else do it, before attempting it yourself. Of course, clipping can be done in the pet shop if you prefer not to do it yourself. This also prevents the bird from associating a bad experience with its new surroundings.

There are two main methods of wing clipping: (1) cutting all the primary feathers or (2) cutting some secondary and all primary feathers except the outer two or three. The latter method preserves the long, graceful appearance of the flight feathers in the resting position.

One or both wings can be clipped. Clipping only one results in the bird losing control over its flight direction. This facilitates taming. The bird is more quickly discouraged from fleeing when it cannot fly where it intends.

If you choose to clip the feathers yourself, support the body of the bird on your lap or a counter. Never hold it by the neck or the tail. Place your thumb under the lower mandible and your second and third fingers around its head. Keep the neck straight without pushing or pulling the head. Use the other fingers to hold the feet and torso. Monitor the bird's respiration. Note any symptoms of distress.

Extend the wing from the bend to get a clear view. Use a pair of barber scissors or small wire cutters for cutting. Cut along the tips of the covert feathers, being sure to trim no closer than one-half inch from the skin. If you cut a growing feather, it may bleed. Having styptic powder on hand to stop the bleeding is a good idea.

Be aware that the flight feathers will be fully regrown in about six months. If you intend to keep the bird clipped, check for new growth periodically.

Taming

Fortunately, Budgerigars are one of the most easily tamed cage birds. Young birds around five to six weeks old are tamed most quickly. Older birds are seldom as friendly and usually more shy. Their taming requires more time and patience. As with any bird, though, the more time invested, the faster the results. Have a fam-

Budgies are very easy to tame. This book will give you some hints, but there are books on how to train your Budgie. Younger birds are much easier to tame than older birds.

ily member with plenty of time and motivation do the initial taming. Give short lessons of 15 to 20 minutes, to keep the bird from over-tiring and losing interest. Give a taming lesson each time the bird is removed from the cage. The more accustomed a bird is to human handling, the easier it will be to train further. Several times every day is suggested. Too much time in between and continuity is lost.

At first, the bird may shiver or avoid your advances. Be patient. Allow the bird a few days to adjust and calm down. Speak to the bird and move closer to the cage. When the bird pays attention to you, stick or hand taming in the cage can begin. Use your own judgment to set the pace. Each bird has its own temperament.

Have one person train the bird. That same person should continue giving the lessons because having one trainer is less confusing for the bird. Only that person should be in the room during the sessions. Remove any toys from the cage. The less extraneous activity there is, the less distraction for the bird.

Speak and whistle softly to the bird to keep it calm. Offer a finger perch to your bird. Press the side of your finger into the breast region of the bird to make it climb onto your finger. If the bird bites, do not make any jerking movements that may frighten it. The bite may pinch, but is rarely harmful. Never hit the bird, just say *No!*

This beautiful bird is very tame, but it is not show quality. The color is cobalt pied. Photo by Harry V. Lacey.

loudly. The bird will soon stop. As a precaution, you can wrap your fingers in adhesive strips or tape. A pair of thin cotton gloves can also be worn. Bulky gloves will make grasping the bird more difficult and will be frightening to it. Sometimes the bird will use its beak to steady itself when climbing. This is not intended as a bite.

The quality of a Budgie as a show
specimen has nothing to do with tameness.

If your bird is a biter, especially a female, stick taming may be preferred. The bird will then grab and gnaw the stick if it bites. The bird may even respond better to a stick when moving it in and out of the cage. Stick taming proceeds the same as hand taming. Then continue on to hand taming. Using a stick can also be used as a handy trick for retrieving the bird from high places.

Once the bird is relaxed on your hand, stroke and scratch it to simulate preening. The bird is now ready for further taming out of the cage.

Most importantly, the bird's wings need to be clipped. This will not detract from its appearance and is painless. Clipping is a helpful aid in training, and the feathers grow back. Taming an unclipped bird is more tiring and frustrating.

Choose a small quiet room, one with little furniture and no high perches. The fewer things there are for the bird to bump into or hide behind will make retrieval that much easier. Make sure there is no escape through an open window or door. Pull the drapes so the bird won't fly into a window, and cover all mirrors. You may want to have a stand ready outside of the cage to place the bird on after a session.

Scatter a few seeds in front of the cage to entice the bird to come out. If it does not come out on its own, bring it out on your finger or a stick.

Work close to the floor by getting on your knees. This prevents long falls. If there is no rug, spread out a towel for traction and to cushion landings. Move slowly and approach the bird from the front. Do not sneak up on the bird from behind and grab it. A frightened bird is not trainable. By not alarming it, the bird will relax and realize no harm is intended.

Due to very successful selective inbreeding, many color varieties of Budgies breed true to a predictable result. This very rare color variety is a recessive pied yellow-wing light green. Photo by Harry V. Lacey.

Budgies do not drink a lot of water . . . most caged birds do not. But the water they do drink is absolutely essential for their lives. Be sure to offer your bird fresh drinking water. A bird bath, like this one, serves two purposes.

Surround the bird from below with outstretched fingers. Now coax it onto your hand. Backing it into a corner may make this easier. Let it perch until calm. Slowly lift your hand from the floor and stand up. This may need to be repeated several times before the bird will remain on your hand. Stroke the bird and praise it.

Food is a useful training tool with Budgies. Reward good behavior and ignore anything else.

Offer a finger perch higher than the other hand. Again, press your finger against its belly to make it step up. This is a new sensation for your bird.

Once the bird is comfortable in your hand, you can coax it to your shoulder. With a rolling motion of your hand, the bird will be forced to step on your shoulder to regain its balance. You may even like to try your head. Just remember, there is no such thing as a housebroken Budgie!

n opaline grey green cock Budgie. Photo by Harry V. Lacey.

This is a yellow-faced skyblue female (hen) with her single chick. Some breeders feel that a pair should raise only one chick at a time.

Budgies are magnificent birds in their natural habitat. They fly long distances for food and water, perhaps covering a thousand miles in a few months. In your home, they can fly equally as well, so be careful that all windows are shut and the doors are not opened unexpectedly . . . or your bird might become lost.

After a session, place the bird on a perch set up outside the cage. If it moves off, simply return the Budgie to it. It will soon remain there.

Return the bird to its cage and offer it plenty of food and water. Your Budgie will probably be tired and thirsty.

Train the bird for longer sessions each day. It will react quickly to attention. To avoid a one-man bird, introduce other family members once it is tame. Have them feed and play with it.

Allowing the Budgie to come out of the cage for exercise will ensure better health and make it friendlier towards people. The bird will fly around to explore, but will probably come back to you with a little encouragement. Feed the Budgie only in its cage so it will return there when hungry. Filling a dish with fresh food is very enticing.

The least you should expect from your bird is to have it rest comfortably on your hand. With the bird feeling safe and secure in your hands, it will be easier to examine and treat it in the future.

If you allow your bird to fly around the house, do not leave anything around worth saving that can be chewed. Always supervise the bird to prevent the gnawing of furniture, plants and wallpaper. Provide plenty of chew toys for distraction.

Budgies have a great sense of play. In advanced training, your pet can be taught simple tricks, such as climbing ladders and ringing bells. The Budgie can perch on pull toys, push and pull objects with its beak, and balance on swings. It may even invent some games of its own for amusement. Check any playstands or toys to ensure that all materials are nonpoisonous, unbreakable, and have no sharp edges. Even natural behavior, like spreading its wings on command, can be reinforced.

Think of advanced training as an extension of the initial training. Use the same room and the same trainer. Short sessions and positive reinforcements of praise and food work best. Do not confuse the bird with too many things at once. Practice one activity until it is mastered, then introduce another.

Talking

Budgerigars are known for their fantastic verbal abilities. They can learn to repeat words, phrases and whistle tunes. Don't be surprised if your bird mimics telephones, doorbells, dogs, and other birds. Of course, talking is not guaranteed, and the length of time it will take your bird to speak is unpredictable. After learning its first word, your Budgie will quickly and unexpectedly pick up other words and sounds, and continually learn over the years. A word to the wise: Be careful what you say around a bird that talks!

Develop a uniform schedule of daily training to facilitate learning. Think of talking as another advanced training trick. Keep the bird in the cage to lessen distraction, and using the same trainer may be helpful. Birds do respond to the high-pitched voices of women and children, though. Most importantly, the bird must be tame and comfortable with its teacher. A rested and relaxed bird will respond more readily, and will probably better imitate someone to whom it is attached.

Fifteen to twenty minutes a day, preferably early morning or in the evening, when it is most attentive is a good amount of time before you lose the bird's interest. Choose simple words and phrases, introducing one at a time until the Budgie repeats it. Speak clearly and slowly, because a bird has a tendency to repeat phrases more quickly than they were taught. A loud voice will get the bird's attention. Do not interject extraneous dialogue.

When the bird repeats the desired sound, keep saying it until the pronunciation is clear. Reward the appropriate speech with a treat. When the bird is fluent, begin something new.

Male Budgies have a wider range of sound, therefore they are better imitators. You may want to buy training tapes or even make one yourself.

A beautiful skyblue Budgie of show quality. Note the large head and the throat dots which are so vivid and huge. Like dogs, cats and horses, just to mention a few domesticated animals, the standards have little to do with the psychological traits which make them better pets. Photo by Harry V. Lacey.

Breeding

Breeding Budgerigars can be a time of excitement or of disappointment. The entire cycle of two months (from laying of the eggs to the weaning of the chicks) may proceed without a hitch, or breeding may not occur at all. If it becomes necessary to hand-rear the chicks, it means a great deal of commitment from you. But the thrill of seeing newborn Budgies is enough for many people to take the chance of mating birds.

Budgies are one of the easiest parrots to breed. Some tame birds, though, will not accept a mate. They are more interested in amusing their owners than settling down to raise a family. Therefore, you may want to keep such birds as pets and buy others for breeding.

Even though Budgies may be fertile at a younger age, birds more than one year old are preferred. Mating related Budgies will concentrate both good and bad features. Home breeders are usually interested in producing color varieties, of which Budgies offer a wide choice.

Since Budgies are not seasonal breeders, they can be brought into breeding condition at any time. A proper diet and a suitable nest are the only necessary provisions. The preferred time for breeding is spring. More seeding grasses and fresh vegetables are available. The longer days mean more hours of light to care for the young. Summer is often too hot, and cold weather increases the chances of birds getting chills.

Poor nutrition can result in egg binding, illness in the breeding pair, and infertile eggs. In such situations, the parents may refuse to, or not be able to, take care of the young.

In addition to the regular diet, special nesting foods are available on the market. Some birds will accept it and others not. To induce them to eat it, introduce it mixed in with their usual seed. Once they are accustomed to it, offer it in a separate dish. The food is very rich and fattening but essential. If the birds receive only seed at this time, the young may be weak, susceptible to disease, and have a shortened life span. You can even make your own combination of soft nesting food in a mixture of hard-boiled eggs, milk powder, dried insects, honey, sugar, powered calcium, vitamins, minerals, and cod-liver oil. During breeding, the consumption of grit and cuttlebone will also increase.

Breeding cage

Budgies do not need much exercise during breeding. A cage at least two feet long, one and a half feet high, and one foot deep is sufficient. Install two perches far enough apart that the birds must fly from one to the other. Place them far enough from the walls that feathers are not damaged.

Keep the floor dry and clean. Clean the cage every day and replenish the food. Leave the birds alone for the rest of the time. Choose a location where there is little disturbance.

When the hen is actually laying the eggs, do not clean the cage. Any disturbance may upset her, so keep your distance.

Nest box

There is little chance of breeding occurring without a proper nest. A nest box can be bought, or you can construct one yourself.

Construct a wooden box about seven inches cubed. Less floor area may be damaging to the eggs or chicks because of the adults stepping on them. Cut a round hole large enough for the birds to fit through, but small enough to afford privacy. This opening should be about two inches from the top to prevent any chicks from being able to climb out too early.

Toward the back of the box, opposite the hole, create a shallow depression, or use a nest frame two inches square, to keep the eggs from rolling. Placing it away from the door lessens the possibility of the adults trampling the eggs as they enter.

Fasten the top with hinges so that the nest box can be opened for cleaning. Place ventilation holes high on the sides.

Cover the bottom with plastic or paper, and then an inch or two of sawdust. The hen will make her own adjustments when it is time for laying. She may remove much of the sawdust, and she may pull some feathers from her breast to line the nest. Her strong beak muscles allow her to chew the box to make changes. To prevent excess chewing, provide her with sticks of soft wood in the nest box.

Hens can have from four to nine eggs . . . and they have the ability to care for and feed that many chicks if you supply them with the correct diet.

Breeding cycle

Most importantly, be sure the birds you have paired are a male and a female. Allow the couple time to get used to each other, then make the nest box available. If the box is introduced too early, the hen may retreat into it and not allow adequate opportunity for mating.

Mating often occurs immediately, but several weeks might elapse. During courtship, the birds engage in a lot of mutual preening. Eventually, the male mounts the female, using his claws to gain a foothold on the female's back. It is for this reason that a lame bird is usually no good for breeding.

If mating has not occurred in three or four weeks, illness may be suspected. Or, a simple change, like a new location or bedding material, can be tried. If all else fails, a new mate is the next choice.

If mating took place but no eggs followed, a new hen is required.

Breeding males do not typically form a strong bond with their mate. They may even be "unfaithful" while the hen is sitting on the eggs. If the eggs are clear, showing no vascularization when held to a light, they are infertile and a new male is needed. However, many hens will not accept a new mate during one season, though the following year a change in mates will be less of a problem.

Prior to laying, the female has a lump on the underside of the tail near the vent. She may look ruffled and bloated. Her breathing is more labored. She remains in the nest box up to eighteen days, laying an egg every other day. There can be anywhere from four to nine pure white eggs in a clutch. The male will feed her during this time. Some males will actually sit with the hen and immediately help with the care of the chicks.

It will take about eighteen days for an egg to hatch. They will hatch in the same order as they were laid, in one- or two-day intervals. Therefore, the chicks will be at different stages of development.

Breeders not only feed the chicks, they also keep them warm and protect them from harm. Leave the breeders alone as much as possible while they are sitting.

Hearing the birds peep will be your first clue that they have hatched. They are born blind and almost naked. Around eight days later they will be covered with gray-white down. In two weeks, plumage colors will be visible.

For the first few days, the hen will feed the young in a unique way. Special glands in the proventriculus secrete a milky substance. Called crop milk, or Budgie milk, it contains fats and proteins. The hen regurgitates this into the mouths of her young. Feeding her nestling food at this time improves the quality of the milk.

The hen regulates the amount of solids and liquid given to each chick. The male joins in to help with the feedings. As the hen prepares to lay a new clutch, he may take full responsibility for the care of the young.

The peeping will get progressively louder, and flapping can be heard inside the nest. As the chicks' feathers grow in, the hen will sleep outside of the box. After around four weeks, the chicks will poke their heads out and examine the cage. They will be fully feathered and practice flying. At night, they will return to the box to sleep.

The chicks are still dependent on their parents for food. In about two weeks more they become completely self-supporting and no longer return to the nest box.

When the chicks are three weeks old, you can begin "pre-taming". Hold them in your hand and stroke gently. Most of the young will sit quietly, but some females may bite.

At three and a half weeks, place canary seed or oatmeal in the nest box to encourage the chicks to eat solid food. After they venture out into the cage, put a dish of food on the floor. Small chicks may not be able to find or reach a hanging dish.

Handle the chicks often, but leave the feeding to the parents. They will probably grow stronger and healthier than with artificial feeding. As long as the chicks are being fed by the parents do not separate them. The chicks are not fully weaned, and by removing them from the breeding cage they will lose weight and become ill. At around six weeks of age the chicks can be moved to a nursery cage.

I wonder what the dog is thinking?

Budgies will breed continuously until they exhaust themselves. There will always be chicks or eggs in the nest box. Do not allow a mating pair to produce more than three clutches in a season. Interrupt breeding at the point when the hen stops feeding and retreats into the nest box. She may not allow the chicks to enter, and may even injure them. This is the time to remove the nest box. Leave both parents in the cage to care for the young.

Illness or aggression in the adults may require the removal of one or both parents. Hand-rearing should not be attempted unless both adults abandon or abuse their young, or if the chicks fail to thrive. If the chicks are older, place them in a nursery cage with another single adult male. He may help to feed them.

If the chicks are too young to feed themselves, hand-rearing is necessary. Place them in an incubator with a steady temperature of 95 degrees until their feathers grow in. Feed them nestling food softened with warm water every three hours for about three weeks. Be sure their crops always contain some food. Use an eyedropper or a small spoon, then wipe the chicks clean with a damp cloth or a cotton swab. Any food that dries on the body can be irritating and cause sores. Hand-reared chicks usually stay dependent longer than other chicks.

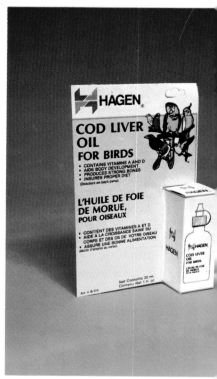

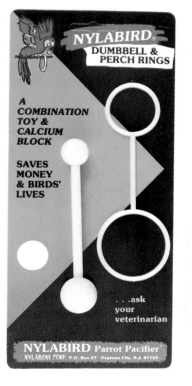

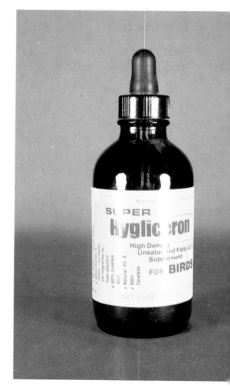

4.

Diseases

Budgerigars are remarkably free from disease. One reason is that their food in captivity is not too different from that in the wild. Of course, accidents and illness can happen, but do not panic. If it is something simple, refer to this book and others, your local petshop salesperson, or a vet. For something more serious, be sure to call a vet.

Your pet dealer will have many remedies
to solve your health and disease problems.
Consult him frequently.

With the right conditions, Budgies are hardy birds and will thrive in captivity. Preventive maintenance is, of course, the most important aspect. A clean cage and the proper diet will make illness unlikely.

Ill birds will sleep on two legs instead of one. There will be a lack of activity and unusually ruffled feathers (in an attempt to conserve body heat). Difficulty maintaining body temperature and a lack of appetite indicate disease. Do not wait long to call a vet, because weight loss can be rapid and fatal.

Isolate sick birds, away from all others, in a hospital cage. You can buy, rent, or make one yourself. Cover all but the front of the regular cage, or a smaller one, with plastic or cloth to prevent drafts and block outside stimulation that may excite the bird. A suspended light bulb or a heating pad will provide additional warmth. A constant temperature of 85 degrees is good.

Remove all perches and place the food and water containers on the floor. Your pet may become fussy about the food it eats, so supply some of its favorites. A balanced diet is still preferred, but getting the bird to eat something is important.

If it is necessary to transport the bird to a vet, keep it quiet and warm. Avoid drastic changes in temperature.

Broken legs and wings

The best idea is to call a vet. The injury may be more serious than it appears. Broken legs require proper splinting and bandaging for healing. If done incorrectly, the bird may be permanently crippled and unable to breed. It will take about two weeks for the bird to recover.

Colds

Symptoms for a cold are similar to other ailments; lethargy, and ruffled feathers, possibly accompanied by sneezing, coughing, or

This is the proper way to hold a Budgie.
Use one hand. Photo by Harry V. Lacey.

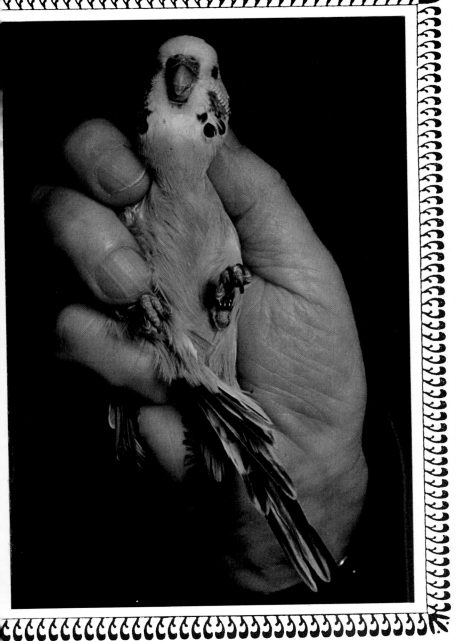

wheezing. The bird may have a nasal discharge and sore-looking eyes. Give weak chamomile tea instead of water and cut out greens and juicy fruits. If the condition persists, call a vet. When not treated properly, the cold can develop into other more complicated and serious conditions, such as pneumonia, asthma, and other chronic and fatal infections.

Conjunctivitis

Your Budgie will shut its eyes often and blink a lot. The eyes will be watery. If the condition worsens daily, see a vet.

Constipation

Your pet will have difficulty passing droppings, which may be small and hard. This is usually the result of an inferior diet. Increase the supply of fresh, leafy vegetables. Your vet may recommend a laxative.

Diarrhea

Diarrhea is often associated with some other ailment. Your bird will sit with ruffled feathers and have a soiled vent from loose, watery droppings. It may also result from an improper diet, or the consumption of unclean food or water. Dehydration can occur quickly because the Budgie retains a small amount of water.

Provide some weak chamomile tea, and remove all fruits and vegetables until the discharge is normal.

Cuts and open wounds

The bleeding will stop quickly if the damage is not severe. Wash the area with hydrogen peroxide and apply styptic powder. If the injury is more critical, consult a vet.

Feather picking

In this condition, the bird plucks its own feathers, which results in bald spots. Sometimes this is due to a diet lacking in mineral content, so adjust the diet. Other causes may be anxiety or boredom. Provide your bird with plenty of toys and attention.

A very nice mauve Budgie. Photo by Harry V. Lacey.

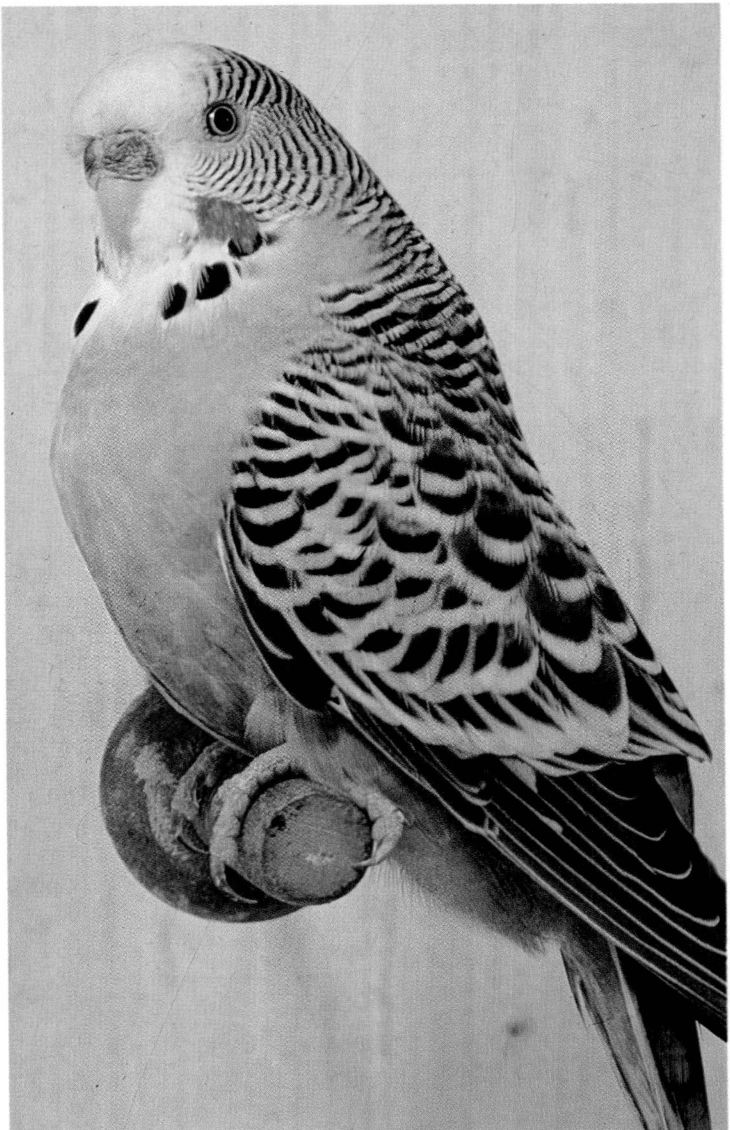

Psittacosis

Psittacosis can be transferred from animals to people. Rare in caged pets, its symptoms in people are similar to pneumonia. If you suspect psittacosis, see a vet immediately.

French molt

French molt results in an unkempt appearance and an inability to fly properly. The wing and tail feathers shed constantly. Since the cause of this disease is unknown, no treatment is available.

Going light

The bird exhibits a marked weight loss. Sometimes this is associated with another illness, sometimes the cause cannot be determined. Provide more fattening foods like oats, sunflower seeds, milk-soaked wheat bread, and corn kernels. Your vet may recommend an appetite stimulant.

Heat stroke

Typically caused by a careless owner who left the bird exposed a long time to direct or very strong reflected sunlight. Spray the bird with cool water or rub with a moist cloth or sponge. Chances of recovery are slim if not treated soon enough.

Indigestion

Vomiting is a sign of some other illness or an improper diet. Act accordingly.

Lice/mites

If your bird scratches a lot, closely examine it and the perch. Mites live in wood and emerge to feed on your bird by sucking blood or chewing feathers.

Disinfect the cage and perches immediately. Scrub with a stiff brush and use commercial preparations available in pet shops. The vet will prescribe a suitable treatment for the bird.

A light green champion Budgie with a peculiar eye problem. Photo by Harry V. Lacey.

Watery eyes

A sign of conjunctivitis or a cold.

Tumors

Appearing as lumps under the skin, tumors are often yellowish. Some are cancerous and result in death. Have them examined by a vet.

Overgrown beaks and claws

Overgrown beaks are rare. They need to be treated very carefully, so it is best to visit a vet. Having cuttlebone and other items for chewing diminishes the chance of occurrence. Overgrown claws are more common and easily treated. Trim with fingernail clippers, a little at a time to avoid cutting a blood vessel. Treat with styptic powder or hydrogen peroxide should bleeding occur. Smooth rough edges with a nail file. Wooden perches help to keep claws trim.

Shock

Usually the result of an injury, the bird stops moving and emits crying sounds, or it may be silent. The eyes do not focus, and the breathing is shallow. Move the bird to a warm, protected spot. You may wrap it in a cloth, and minimize disturbances. Put food and water within reach and check for an injury that may need attention. It may take a while for the bird to respond; meanwhile, leave it to rest.

Ingrown feathers

These appear as lumps at the base of the feather follicles. As the feathers grow but can't poke through the skin, the lumps grow larger. Have this treated by a vet.

Arthritis and rheumatism

Often the result of wet perches or perches that are too small in diameter for a proper grip. The best prevention is a variety of perches of various diameters.

Lameness or sore feet

Soak the feet in warm water or under a light stream of running water for five minutes. Do not get the rest of the bird wet. Dress the feet with iodine or mercurochrome and leave uncovered.

The following books are available from your petshop. Petshops carry a full range of pet books; they also have a lot of knowledge not to be found in books.

BUDGERIGAR HANDBOOK
By Ernest H. Hart
ISBN 0-87666-414-1; **TFH H-901**

Contents: Forming A Stud. Modes Of Inheritance. Basic Breeding Techniques. The Mechanics of Breeding. Aviaries And Equipment. Feeding And Management. Selection And Upgrading. Trouble Hints And Ailments. Shows And The Standard. Matings And Color Expectation. Training The Pet Budgerigar. The Future.
Audience: This is the most complete book on the subject of budgerigars (parakeets). Almost every color variety is shown in full color photographs, and showing, breeding, and every subject of importance for the budgerigar enthusiast is completely covered.
Hard cover, 5½ x 8½", 251 pages 67 black and white photos, 104 color photos.

TRAINING BUDGERIGARS TO TALK
By Opal Dunigan
ISBN 0-87666-845-7; **TFH PS-791**

Contents: Selecting a Budgerigar. General Care. Training a Male Budgerigar. Female Budgerigars. Adventures with Pissel.
Audiences: This down-to-earth text will be of value to any budgie enthusiast. Step by step the author explains the methods used to turn budgerigars into more than just ornamental pets. Following her directions, the bird owner may acquire a companion who is also a bit of a comedian and entertainer.
Hard cover, 5½ x 8", 128 pages 40 full color photos, 64 black and white.

ENCYCLOPEDIA OF BUDGERIGARS
By Georg Radtke
ISBN 0-87666-899-6; **TFH H-1027**

Contents: Care and Breeding. Disease Prevention and Treatment. Care and Training of House Pets. Selective Breeding. The British Show Budgerigars. Color Varieties—Their Origin and Development.
Audience: This book has been written for the many, many thousands of owners of budgerigars who have been captivated by their birds to the point that they want a good body of truly detailed and highly authoritative information. This book provides exactly what they're looking for, and it provides it in an eminently readable and painstakingly thorough style. The goodness of the text is matched by the eye-appeal and identification value of the many full-color photos of budgies in a wide range of forms and color variations.
Hard cover, 5½ x 8", 320 pages 148 full-color photos, 44 black and white.

ALL ABOUT BREEDING BUDGERIGARS
By Mervin F. Roberts
ISBN 0-87666-568-7; **TFH PS-804**

Audience: Novice budgie owners who want to start their own breeding programs and veteran budgie breeders who need information on how to improve what they've started will derive great benefit from this practical, useful (and highly colorful) book.
Hard cover, 5½ x 8", 96 pages Illustrated with almost 50 full-color photos, over 20 black and white photo.